D1244287

COUNTRY LIFE
PICTURE BOOK OF
YORKSHIRE

THE TOWERS OF YORK MINSTER FROM THE CITY WALLS

THE COUNTRY LIFE

PICTURE BOOK OF

YORKSIIIRE

COUNTRY LIFE LIMITED LONDON

First published in 1957
by Country Life Limited
Tavistock Street London WC2
Printed and bound in Great Britain by
Hazell Watson & Viney Ltd
Aylesbury & London

LIST OF PLATES

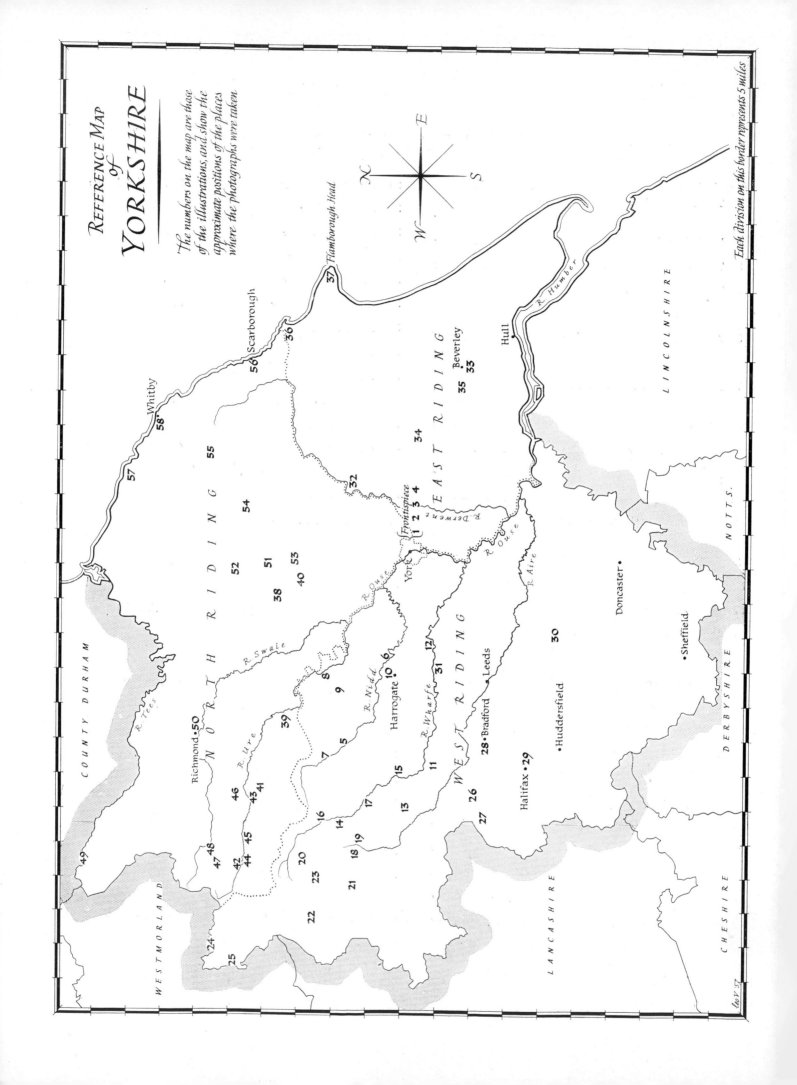

1. MONK BAR, YORK. The medieval walls of the city, over two miles in circumference, were pierced by four chief Bars or Gates —Bootham, Monk, Walmgate and Micklegate—all of which may still be seen to-day.

2. THE MINSTER FROM LOW PETERGATE.   The 'Cathedral and Metropolitan Church of St. Peter', to give the Minster its
full name, is one of the most magnificent examples of Gothic architecture in Europe.

3. THE MINSTER CHOIR.   The original Norman Choir was rebuilt by Archbishop Roger in the middle of the 12th century and then gradually replaced by the present one between the years 1360 and 1405.

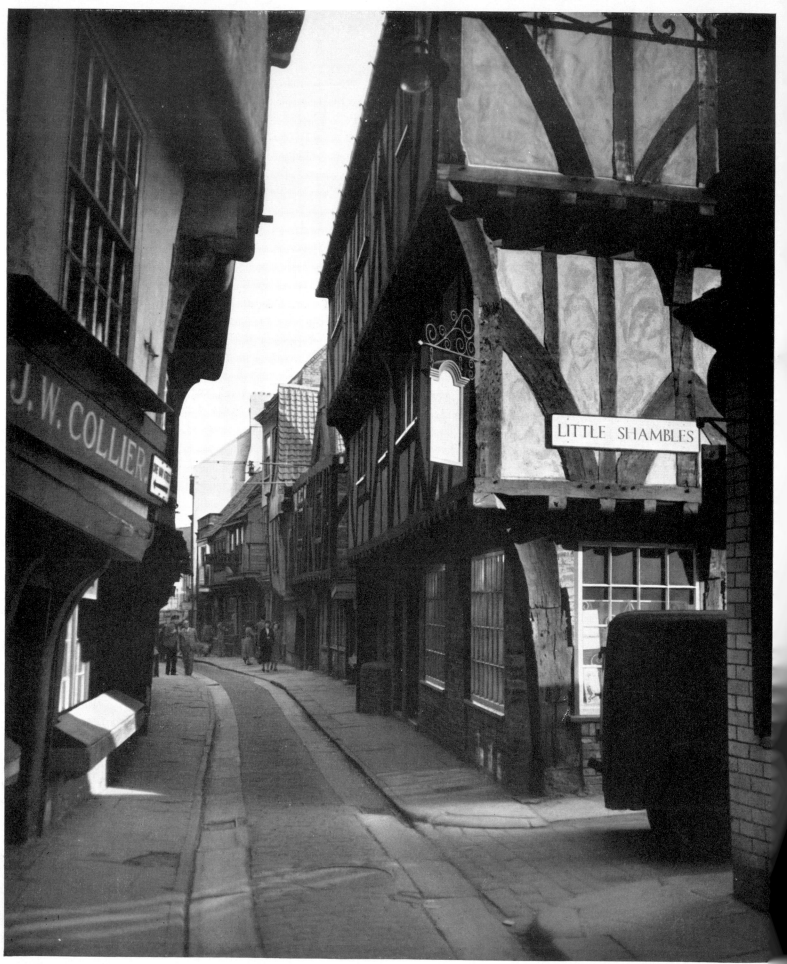

4. THE SHAMBLES. As its curious name suggests, this narrow, crooked street in the centre of the city, with its gabled, overhanging houses, was originally in medieval times famous for its butchers' shops.

5. A WEST RIDING MOORLAND ROAD. This long stretch of road over open moorland scenery north of Pateley Bridge calls to mind Alfred Noyes's poem, *The Highwayman*—'The road was a ribbon of moonlight over the purple moor'.

6. KNARESBOROUGH. Seventeen miles north-west of York is this picturesque town standing high above the River Nidd. It possesses an historic castle, 'Mother Shipton's Cave,' and a famous wishing-well.

7. RAMSGILL AND BOUTHWAITE, NIDDERDALE. Ramsgill will for ever be remembered as the birthplace of Eugene Aram, the 18th-century schoolmaster who was executed for murder and who was the subject of Lord Lytton's novel and Hood's poem.

8. RIPON. A corner of the market square of this small, attractive Cathedral city. Ripon has been a seat of the Church from the days of the northern saints, the first Abbot being St. Wilfrid, to whom the Cathedral is dedicated.

9. FOUNTAINS ABBEY. Three miles from Ripon is this Abbey, founded in 1132 and for four centuries the greatest Cistercian house in the country. The 'great cloisters', vaulted with two aisles, are 300 feet long.

10. HARROGATE. A lighted Christmas Tree outside the floodlit Royal Baths. Harrogate, sometimes called the seaside without the sea, has been a renowned spa since the 18th century, but its health-giving waters were known much earlier.

11. **ILKLEY.** Once a Roman garrison town, Ilkley is now a popular holiday centre. It is seen here from the moor, from which the famous West Riding 'National Anthem'—'On Ilkla Moor baht 'at'—took its name.

12. THE WHARFE AT LINTON, NEAR WETHERBY. A ripple on the surface and the reflection of the sun on the water give a silvery sheen to one of Yorkshire's chief rivers which rise in the Pennines.

13. IN UPPER WHARFEDALE. Sunlight and shadow on a road near Skipton. Below road level the river winds its way in and out of the countryside which is among the wildest in the West Riding.

14. **KILNSEY CRAG.** Eleven miles north of Skipton, this great limestone cliff, originally formed by glacial action, stands 170 feet high above the green of the surrounding country. The hamlet of Kilnsey was mentioned in Domesday Book.

15. **BOLTON ABBEY.** Beautifully situated on the banks of the Wharfe, between Skipton and Ilkley, are the ruins of what should strictly be called Bolton Priory, an Augustinian foundation of the early 12th century.

16. KETTLEWELL. This Upper Wharfedale village, once a busy little market town, is said to take its name from Ketel, an Irish-Norse chieftain, who owned the land before the Norman Conquest. Note the typical rough stone walls.

17. BURNSALL. A five-arched stone bridge spans the Wharfe at this delightful village, which is situated in the same stretch of country as Kettlewell. Wordsworth, Ruskin, Turner and Landseer all knew and loved this beautiful valley.

18. **MALHAM COVE.** It was the scenery around this semicircle of limestone cliff, about 300 feet high, at the base of which the River Aire flows out from a subterranean passage, which inspired Charles Kingsley to write *The Water Babies*.

19. GORDALE SCAR. A little over a mile from Malham Cove, this wild ravine, where cliffs of nearly 400 feet in height overhang a double waterfall, is one of the most sensational and awe-inspiring features of Malhamdale.

20. DEEP IN RIBBLESDALE. Lowering skies, a trace of mist and the lone, wind-twisted tree give the impression of a painting to this scene near the village of Langcliffe, a mile or two north of Settle.

21. **HALTON GILL, LITTONDALE.** This tiny grey stone village, dwarfed by a dark and almost surrealistic background of porous limestone rock, is ten miles north-east of Settle. Littondale joins the valley of the Wharfe at Arncliffe.

22. INGLEBOROUGH. Looking across the rough stone walls, in the limestone country of Ribblesdale, towards the western slopes of Ingleborough, on the broad, flat top of which warning beacons were lit in former times.

23. **PENYGHENT.** Directly across the valley of the Ribble from Ingleborough is Penyghent (2273 feet), the highest point in the Pennine range. From its summit, on a clear day, Helvellyn can be seen.

24. CAUTLEY SPOUT. Water cascading down the rocky sides of one of Yorkshire's famous falls—called Spouts, Snouts or Forces. The village of Cautley is three miles north-east of Sedbergh, site of the ancient public school.

25. THE RIVER LUNE. Reflected in the clear waters of the river, just west of Sedbergh, are cumulus clouds suggestive of a hot summer's day. This is the far north-west corner of Yorkshire, on the Westmorland border.

26. HAWORTH PARSONAGE. Weather-worn gravestones in the churchyard extend to the wall of the Parsonage, home of the Brontës, which is now the Brontë Museum. The Rev. Patrick Brontë brought his family here in 1820.

27. HAWORTH AND THE SURROUNDING COUNTRY. The neighbourhood of Haworth is rich in Brontë associations—Withens ('Wuthering Heights'), Ponden House ('Thrushcross Grange'), Wycoller Hall ('Ferndean Manor'), Stonegappe ('Gateshead Hall').

28. BRADFORD MILLS. It is hard to realise when looking at this air picture of the woollen mills—Bradford is the centre of the wool trade of the world—that the open, bracing moors are within easy reach.

29. HALIFAX. With Bradford (seven miles away), Leeds (sixteen miles away) and Huddersfield (ten miles away), Halifax forms a great manufacturing belt in the West Riding, important for woollens, worsteds, coal, iron, steel and other industries.

30. NOSTELL PRIORY. A fine example of a Chippendale writing-desk in the library designed by Robert Adam. Begun in 1735, this famous country house lies five miles south-east of Wakefield.

31. **HAREWOOD HOUSE.** This equally famous 18th-century house, between Harrogate and Leeds, is owned by the Earl of Harewood, elder son of the Princess Royal. The formal terraced gardens were laid out by Sir Charles Barry.

32. KIRKHAM PRIORY. Six miles south-west of Malton, and just in the East Riding, are the ruins of this 12th-century Augustinian Priory, situated picturesquely on the banks of the River Derwent.

33. BEVERLEY MINSTER. A detail of the exquisitely carved Percy Tomb in the Minster, dating from the 14th century. The Gothic Minster dominates the ancient town of Beverley, which is the capital of the East Riding.

34. COTTAGES AT WARTER. This row of whitewashed, thatched and gabled cottages, standing on a grassy bank and untypical of Yorkshire, are in the little village of Warter, in the crescent formed by the Wolds.

35. BURTON CONSTABLE. This is the magnificent Long Gallery, which occupies the whole of the upper floor of the west front, added to this great Elizabethan house in 1736. Burton Constable lies about seven miles north-east of Hull.

36. FILEY BAY. The sands at this popular seaside resort are not often as deserted as they are in this air photograph. To the north-east of the town is the curiously shaped rocky spit called Filey Brigg.

37. **FLAMBOROUGH HEAD.** This promontory forms the northern horn of Bridlington Bay. The 80-foot lighthouse stands 214 feet above sea-level, and the steep chalk cliffs are a great breeding-place for sea birds.

38. THE PLAIN OF YORK.   A panoramic view from Sutton Bank, east of Thirsk, in the North Riding.   Several tributaries of the Ouse-Humber river system—the Swale, Ure, Nidd, Wharfe, Aire and Calder—converge in this area.

39. MASHAM. On the river Ure, some eight miles north-west of Ripon, is Masham, a small town which has a large and picturesque market-place. Four miles away are the ruins of the Cistercian Abbey of Jervaulx.

40. COXWOLD. The wide street of this enchanting village, where Laurence Sterne was curate from 1760–68 and where, in the house called Shandy Hall, he wrote part of *Tristram Shandy* and *A Sentimental Journey*.

41. PENHILL, WENSLEYDALE. The valley of the River Ure, Wensleydale contains some of the finest scenery in the North Riding. Penhill, seen here across a sweep of country, is a gritstone ridge rising to 1685 feet.

42. HARDRAW FORCE.   Some idea of the height (about 95 feet) of this famous Wensleydale waterfall may be gained from the figure of the man standing just to the right of the fall.

43. THE LOWER FALLS, AYSGARTH. Equally beautiful as Hardraw Force, though less spectacular, are the Aysgarth Falls caused by the River Ure flowing over a series of flat limestone ledges.

44. HAWES, WENSLEYDALE.   The footpath leading to the church at Hawes, in Upper Wensleydale, a small grey town with narrow streets, that is the marketing centre for the farms lying around and a popular centre for walkers.

45. THE HORNBLOWER. At Bainbridge, a few miles from Hawes, may be seen this famous horn which used to be sounded on winter nights to guide travellers when mists were threatening on the surrounding fells.

46. BOLTON CASTLE, WENSLEYDALE. Built in the 14th century, this mighty castle was the stronghold of the Scropes, Wardens of the Western Marches, for three hundred years. Mary Queen of Scots was imprisoned here in 1568.

47. BUTTERTUBS. This rather desolate-looking pass, running for five and a half miles and rising to 1726 feet, connects Hawes, in Wensleydale, with Muker in Swaledale. The 'Buttertubs' themselves are deep holes in the limestone rock.

48. MUKER IN SWALEDALE. After the long pull over the Buttertubs Pass, the traveller would be glad to reach Muker, even if it were not one of the most picturesque and most photographed villages in the North Riding.

49. HIGH FORCE, TEESDALE. The small figure of a man is outlined against the sky in this picture of the much-visited waterfall, where the River Tees plunges over a basalt cliff seventy-two feet in height.

50. RICHMOND CASTLE. This air photograph shows the strategic situation of the ancient castle—begun only five years after the Norman Conquest by the first Earl of Richmond—on a cliff high above the River Swale.

51. RIEVAULX ABBEY. In Ryedale are the majestic ruins of Rievaulx, a Cistercian house, built some sixty years later than Richmond Castle. The most celebrated Abbot was St. Aelred, the 12th-century historian.

52. RYEDALE AND EASTERSIDE. The word Rievaulx means 'valley of the Rye' and, being within easy reach of the little town of Helmsley and containing superb scenery, the dale is very attractive to walkers.

53. AMPLEFORTH COLLEGE. A few miles south of Helmsley and Kirkby (pronounced 'Kirby') Moorside stands one of Yorkshire's famous public schools. Others are Sedbergh, Giggleswick and St. Peter's, York, originally founded in the year 627.

54. HUTTON-LE-HOLE. On the edge of the moors, three or four miles from Kirkby Moorside, are the charming villages of Lastingham and Hutton-le-Hole. The road passes alongside the moorland stream that runs through the village.

55. ELLER BECK, GOATHLAND. Hutton-le-Hole is on the south edge of the moors, Goathland is on the north, some eight miles from Whitby. This rushing moorland stream is typical of many in the North Riding.

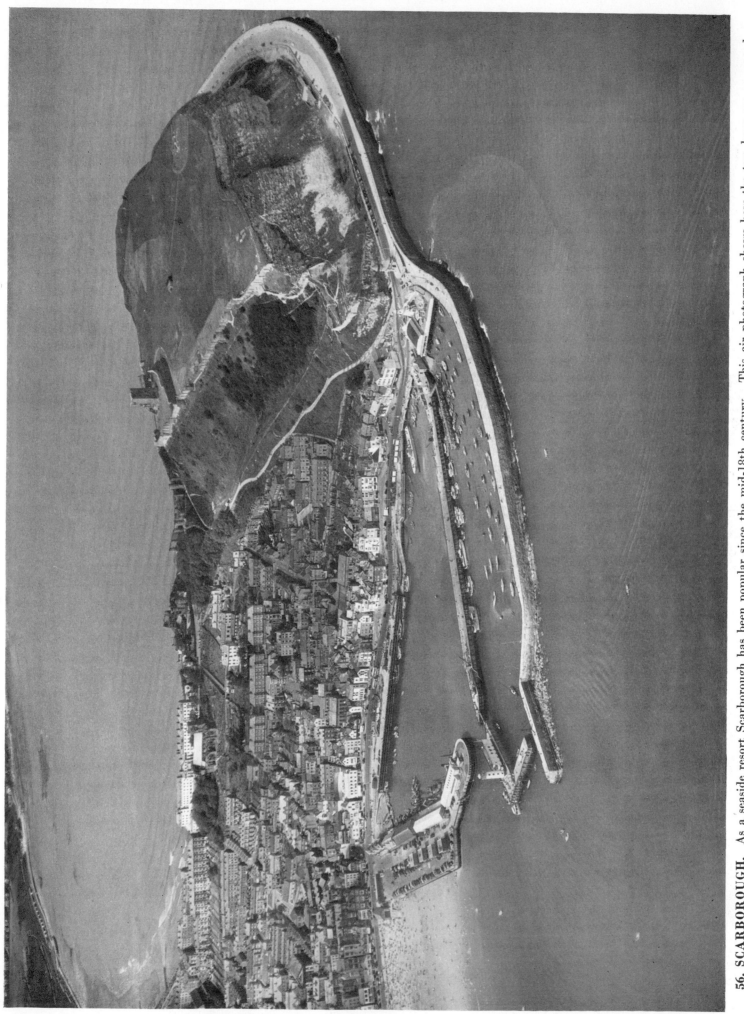

56. SCARBOROUGH. As a seaside resort Scarborough has been popular since the mid-18th century. This air photograph shows how the two bays are separated by a rocky eminence crowned by the ruins of the old castle.

57. STAITHES AND BOULBY CLIFF. This fishing village has preserved much of the same character that it had in the days when the future Captain Cook worked there as a boy. Boulby Cliff rises beyond Staithes to a height of 666 feet.

58. SUNSET OVER WHITBY. Now a popular seaside resort, Whitby is one of the most historic towns in England, the scene in A.D. 664 of the synod at which England acknowledged the authority of the Church of Rome.